JESUS, GUIDE *of My* LIFE

"In this most recent addition to her series of Lenten reflections, Sr. Joyce Rupp incisively fixes our attention on the Jesus who is the Way to Easter life. She exposes aspects of Christ-centered scriptures that may have escaped previous notice and that should burrow in our souls in places where the Spirit can bring healing, integration, and newfound hope. I highly commend this resource as a staple and prayer primer in the hidden 'room' we dare to enter in this graced season and beyond."

Most Rev. William M. Joensen
Bishop of Des Moines

"My soul says yes to this Lenten devotional. Joyce Rupp's balance of scripture, personal reflection, prayer, and action nourished me in a way that regrounded me in my yes to living the Way."

timone davis, DMin
Professor of Pastoral Theology at Loyola University Chicago

"In a day and age when conflicting ideological views abound over what it means to be a Christian, we can count on Joyce Rupp to point us back to our foundation: the life and teaching of Jesus. Rupp has done it again in *Jesus, Guide of My Life*, and we will find rest for our weary souls."

Shannon K. Evans
Spirituality editor at *National Catholic Reporter* and author of *Feminist Prayers for My Daughter*

REFLECTIONS *for the* LENTEN JOURNEY

JESUS,
GUIDE
of My
LIFE

JOYCE RUPP

AVE MARIA PRESS AVE Notre Dame, Indiana

_____

© 2023 by Joyce Rupp

Founded in 1865, Ave Maria Press is a ministry of the United States Province of Holy Cross.

www.avemariapress.com

Paperback: ISBN-13 978-1-64680-285-2

E-book: ISBN-13 978-1-64680-286-9

Cover image © GettyImages.com.

Cover design by Samantha Watson.

Text design by Brian C. Conley.

Printed and bound in the United States of America.

Contents

Introduction

Come to me. . . . Learn from me.
—Matthew 11:28–29

When I pause to consider what guides the flow of my life, the teachings of Jesus in the Christian gospels are center stage. These transformative messages continue to provide counsel and direction for how I am to live. I cannot imagine a spiritual journey without its being based on these foundational principles. Many a time I've neglected their directives. At other times I have given them ample attention and activation. Each Lent I return to their guidance. When I do so, I see that some of what I think, say, and do has to be restored to its true and solid footing. I gladly welcome a fresh slant or insight that regrounds my spiritual growth. This sighting enlivens my motivation to faithfully follow what the gospels encourage for ongoing transformation. I hope this will be your experience with *Jesus, Guide of My Life*.

Already in his early years Jesus revealed an interest in how biblical texts could be a source of personal

1

guidance. At twelve years old he sat in the Temple among the scholarly rabbis "listening to them and asking them questions" (Lk 2:46). Eighteen years later he entered the public sphere and soon became a prominent and respected teacher who inspired many to embrace his message. To the very end of his life, Jesus remained a guide of minds and director of hearts, even offering counsel in his dying hours: "Father, forgive them; for they do not know what they are doing" (Lk 23:34).

The teachings of Jesus thread through every aspect of human life. They pilot us when we are caught in the stormy weather of grief and serve as guardrails when our minds travel on roads made of worry and self-deprecation. His wise precepts direct us to release our failures and be aware of our shortcomings. His wisdom enables us to make judicious decisions when we are at a difficult crossroads. His reassurance gives us courage to choose what is good and become ever more loving human beings.

"I AM THE WAY"

When Jesus steps onto the landscape of his public ministry, he does so as a teacher, healer, and counselor whose central message is always about "the way"—the path by which to abide more intently and profoundly in the kingdom of God, the realm of divine love. In *The Last Week*, scripture scholars Marcus Borg and John Dominic Crossan remind their readers that "the Greek word for 'way' is *hodos* . . . translated with a number of words: 'way,' 'road,' 'path.' Mark's Gospel opens by referring to 'the way,' telling of a messenger (John the Baptist) who will come 'to prepare *the way* of the Lord'"[1] (see Mk 1:2–3).

Gradually, the disciples who follow, and the crowds that gather, come to recognize that this "way" is more than a directional path. Jesus is not only guiding them on their interior road; he is the very embodiment of that guidance: he *is* the Way (see Jn 14:6). Author Marilyn McEntyre writes, "Remember that *The Way* is a person."[2] Episcopal priest Vincent Pizzuto expresses something similar: "Christ, who said, 'I am the Way,' is for us the wayless Way, the path that is a person, the method that is a relationship."[3]

And so it is that the teachings, advice, and counseling of Jesus, who is the Way, lead and direct us on a transforming route that brings us ever further into the fullness of who we truly are—persons capable of great love. This relationship continually widens and deepens as the guidance of the Way becomes intertwined with our everyday comings and goings.

Receiving Guidance

We can be guided anywhere, anytime, by the teachings of Jesus. The variety of situations and places in which he taught long ago indicate this: a stretch of level ground, in the Temple, on a hillside, in the boat, by the lake, in a village, through a field of grain, in the large city of Jerusalem, in homes of the wealthy, and on roadsides with the poor.

Wherever he was, Jesus spent a significant amount of energy giving advice on our attitudes regarding one another: consider others as precious as yourself; cease comparing; be humble and forget about pushing into first place; remember what genuine love is about; move toward rather than away from those who treat you as an enemy; be willing to pay the price for what you believe and value; stand with and support marginalized persons; don't think twice about letting go of what holds you back from being truly kindhearted. These are just a few of the guidelines that inspire and urge me to keep growing, to continue to embrace the directives at the heart of the gospels.

As I meditated on the scripture passages and prepared the reflections in *Jesus, Guide of My Life,* I discovered some common gestures of our beloved counselor:

- *Showing* love and concern as a caring teacher
- *Teaching* how to live into the fullness of his message
- *Testifying* to sacred realities invisible on the surface
- *Pointing* to what one needs to learn and trust
- *Forgiving* those who stumble and fall off of the path
- *Encouraging* the effort to go an extra mile for others
- *Explaining* what human minds find difficult to perceive
- *Leading* into the depths of being where the true self resides
- *Extending* compassion for sorrows, defeats, and struggles
- *Attending* a desire to be a truly loving individual
- *Understanding* how challenging it is to absorb his teachings

- *Cautioning* to stay alert and appreciate life to the utmost
- *Influencing* the decision to be generous and self-giving
- *Finding* the lost when they wander far from the Way
- *Inviting* to accept with faith what is not fully perceived
- *Midwifing* the ongoing process of transformation

Not only can we relate to these gestures of Jesus; they also motivate us to embrace and emulate the Way. Our thoughts, words, and deeds are influenced by what Jesus taught and how he related to others. We know how to live as persons of great love because he has been there before us as our friend, companion, and guide.

ENTERING LENT

"Again he began to teach beside the sea. Such a very large crowd gathered around him that he got into a boat on the sea and sat there, while the whole crowd was beside the sea on the land. He began to teach them many things" (Mk 4:1–2a).

As you move through these Lenten reflections, envision yourself there among the crowd, gathered around Jesus, focusing on what he is teaching. Draw inspiration and courage from knowing others are there with you. Breathe in the kinship you have with them. Like you, each one hopes to grow spiritually, to become more loving, just, and authentic.

Let the words of St. Richard of Chichester's prayer be yours as you walk through Lent:

May we know you more clearly,
love you more dearly,
and follow you more nearly,
day by day.[4]

May this be your intent as you give yourself to these life-changing forty days, guided by the One who is the Way.

ASH WEDNESDAY TO FIRST SUNDAY OF LENT

SELL WHAT YOU OWN

As he was setting out on a journey, a man ran up and knelt before him, and asked him, "Good Teacher, what must I do to inherit eternal life?" . . . Jesus, looking at him, loved him and said, "You lack one thing: go, sell what you own, and give the money to the poor, and you will have treasure in heaven; then come, follow me." When he heard this, he was shocked and went away grieving, for he had many possessions.

—Mark 10:17, 21–22

Usually I have one thing in mind for what I intend to do for Lent to strengthen my alignment with the Way. But then something more efficacious comes along, pointing to what I really ought to do. At first, I want to hold on to my possession—my chosen Lenten practice. For example, as Lent begins, I might decide to be more disciplined by "giving up" something I enjoy, but I work near a person whose constant complaining grates on my nerves. I imagine Jesus saying, "Give away your love to this person. Then come, follow me." Everything in me longs to hoard my possession—my kindness. Who wants to reach out and be friendly, receiving nothing in return, to be generous of spirit when it is easier to turn away? I would much rather choose to pass by that nice dark-chocolate bar urging me to "take a bite," because it requires less of me than to hand over kindness. But my true spiritual practice beckons.

What "possession" do you fiercely cling to that could be shared this Lent? Will you give it away?

Guide of My Life,
expand my heart; open my mind
to know how best to grow spiritually
as I begin to pray my way through Lent.
I desire to let go of whatever keeps me
from living your teachings more fully.

Today: I decide on a spiritual practice that I will
tend during Lent.

Thursday

Restored Awareness

Do not judge, and you will not be judged; do
not condemn, and you will not be condemned.
—Luke 6:37

Judgments weasel their way into my cloudy mind without my noticing them. Convincing assumptions and conclusive verdicts sneak in, bringing unfair or undeserving thoughts. These conclusions often arise due to haughty comparisons and a better-than-thou attitude. One Ash Wednesday, those of us present were squeezed tightly into the pews at Mass, the crowd about as large as that of Christmas. The couple next to me never opened a songbook or offered any verbal responses to the prayers. In front of me sat a middle-aged man with a woman next to him who continually leaned over, whispered in his ear, and smiled coquettishly at him. My disapproving mind wondered, "Why are you here?" and wished they had not taken up space in the packed pews.

The next morning I found an answer to that judgmental question when I opened my prayer book and read the above scripture verse from Luke about not condemning others. Right there I had my Lenten comeuppance: *Who was I to decide why someone else was present at the liturgy? Wasn't it great that they made the effort to be there? And how arrogant of me to presume what their motivations were.* With this renewed awareness of watching my thoughts, I returned to the trust that there's often something positive veiled in what I view as unwanted. That view became my Lenten practice and helped me keep a close eye on my interior judgmental comments.

Open-Minded Guide,
when I think my opinions and actions
are more worthy than those of others,
steer me away from my stony judgments.
Loosen my grip on deciding that everyone
has to be in accord with my personal views.

Today: I attend to unfair, judgmental thoughts
and feelings when they arise.

Friday

SUPPORTING THE WORK OF OTHERS

> Soon afterwards he went on through cities and
> villages, proclaiming and bringing the good
> news of the kingdom of God. The twelve were
> with him, as well as some women . . . who pro-
> vided for them out of their resources.
>
> —Luke 8:1–3

Could Jesus have managed to do so much good in the short
span of his ministry without the substantial contributions
of the women who journeyed with him? Probably not.
Other followers were drawn to the inspiring presence
of Jesus and appreciated his dedicated teaching and
compassionate healing. But the women who shared their
resources to support Jesus did more than marvel about
him. They put their inspiration into action. Supportive
generosity poured forth from their financial coffers

because, as Brother Guy Consolmagno, SJ, has noted, "Those we love, we love to serve."[1] By providing for Jesus and his disciples, the women's assistance ensured that his transformative, profound ministry would continue.

It doesn't take long to locate a nonprofit organization whose goal centers on such tasks as alleviating poverty, developing educational programs, welcoming refugees, or working to change systems responsible for social injustices. Who and what inspire you to provide some of your monetary resources for the sake of people intent on engaging directly with the works of mercy? Almsgiving remains as vital today as in the time of Jesus. Even the smallest contribution makes a difference and affirms the beneficial work of persons engaged with nonprofit organizations. Each donation helps to ensure that compassionate care will be provided and issues of inequality will continue to be addressed.

Itinerant Traveler,
the women who lovingly accompanied you
are a tribute to the compassionate efficacy
of resources freely shared to support others.
I, too, can be generous with what I have
and aid those who engage in works of mercy.

Today: I give a donation to a nonprofit
organization.

Saturday

Pray in Secret

But whenever you pray, go into your room and
shut the door.

—Matthew 6:6a

This morning before dawn I sleepily lit a candle, sat
down, looked out the window to the east, and saw nothing but darkness. I asked myself: "Why do I do this? Why
am I here? What gets me up every day?" The response
came quickly: "Because here you find direction for your
day, strength to enter troubles, comfort for what hurts,
satisfaction and assurance to be once again united with
the Love who claims your heart." I was glad for this
response. It felt accurate about my reason and desire for
daily prayer.

Some people pray best when they are *not* in their private room behind a shut door. These persons with extro-
verted personalities experience insight and guidance
related to spiritual growth when they are more actively

involved. Maybe it's going for a walk, a run, or a swim, or engaging some bodily movement with gestures such as bird-watching, drawing, or painting. None of us can judge how another chooses to pray or where they most readily unite with the One who draws them inwardly. The room we pray in might not be a physical space, but it is always related to the room of our heart. The vital word in Jesus's counsel to pray is *go*—go make an effort to be present with the Holy One every day, whether that is in one's own room, in nature, or while listening to an inspiring song.

Center of My Life,
you know more than I even know myself
how much I desire to be at home with you.
When I am hesitant to pray or when I question
the meager worth or quality of my efforts,
urge me onward with assurance of your love.

Today: I pray in a "room" that supports my unity
with the Holy One.

FIRST WEEK OF LENT

Sunday

TEMPTED

> Jesus, full of the Holy Spirit, returned from the
> Jordan and was led by the Spirit in the wilder-
> ness where for forty days he was tempted by
> the devil.
>
> —Luke 4:1–2a

We are not alone in being tempted away from what is true and good. By his responses during the forty days in the wilderness, Jesus guides us to face our own false enticements. He knew the necessity for a keen perception of what was happening interiorly. The solitude provided Jesus with the opportunity to clarify and purify his reasons for going forth to his ministry. He had to wrestle with his demons, the strong voice of the ego urging a move toward self-glory and dominating power. It was necessary that he be aware of what might tempt him toward these things. Being successful could have swollen his pride out of all proportion. Jesus might have left those forty days with a focus on himself instead of on the people he would be interacting with.

We also meet temptations and false attractions. No matter our age or way of life, we confront harmful decoys in our thoughts and attitudes, such as, "I'm right and you're wrong; I have more money than you do; I'm more attractive than you are." Just as Jesus was "led by the Spirit," so we have this gift of discernment available to us. With this guiding presence, we are able to recognize and stand up to whatever tries to yank us away from a Christlike approach to living.

Discerning Spirit,
when temptations away from good
gather near with their hungry claws,
I will turn to you with alert confidence.
I'll lean heavily on your assured guidance
to help me overcome false enticements.

Today: I watch for what tries to tempt me away
from being my truest self.

Monday

TAKE UP THE CROSS DAILY

Now large crowds were traveling with him;
and he turned and said to them . . . "Whoever
does not carry the cross and follow me cannot
be my disciple."

—Luke 14:25, 27

What did the crowd following Jesus think when he made
that tough statement? Did they wonder what carrying
the cross meant? Did they have second thoughts about
accompanying him? Jesus wanted his followers to know
that the journey they would make involved knowing and
enlivening the teachings he advocated. In other words,
Jesus was cautioning them, "If you decide to give your-
selves to what truly counts in this life, it will cost you. You
will feel these teachings to be burdensome at times, like
the weight of a cross."

We can't just sit on the roadside of life and call ourselves followers of Jesus. We are to do more than esteem

him for his generous love and dedicated service. We do not hear Jesus grumbling about the challenges and demands of this way of life. We do not see him "talking a good talk" but doing nothing about it. He describes his vision and then encourages others to join him in moving those teachings into action. That's the hard part, isn't it? Deciding how much we endeavor to participate in living a Christlike life. The cross can grow heavy. It's tempting to set it down and forget it. Sometimes we do that for a while. Lent has six weeks in which to pick up the cross again and follow. Let's do it.

Companion on My Road of Life,
"Follow me," you say, but then you add,
"This will not always be comfortable for you."
You know my heart. You know my wanderings.
I will free myself from excessive preoccupations
so I can give myself to you more completely.

Today: I take up the cross today by undertaking a
gospel mandate.

Tuesday

MOVING ON

"Let the little children come to me. . . ." And he
laid his hands on them and went on his way.
—Matthew 19:14–15

Jesus guides by his example in this scene. He welcomes
the young ones, deliberately draws them near, and gifts
them with his attentiveness. He intentionally gives of
himself, allowing his loving-kindness to touch them.
After blessing the children, Jesus does not linger to see if
his presence will have a lasting effect on their future. He
moves on, setting aside the desire to know if his kindness
created a permanent influence on the children.

I need to be reminded of this. When leading retreats,
speaking at conferences, visiting the sick, or being involved
in other kinds of service, I do not know if my engagement
will have made a lasting difference. Most people find
themselves in comparable situations. Whether they freely
choose their service or do it out of duty and responsibility,

they invest themselves in their caring and concern, giving what they can to instill a positive influence. Parents do their utmost day after day to raise children to be honorable human beings; teachers diligently encourage students to learn; pastors give tirelessly to assist parishioners; clerks extend kindhearted assistance to customers; peace-and-justice advocates work determinedly for change. All of us invest our presence and talents without the surety of positive outcomes. Like Jesus, we cannot cling to certitude after we have done our best in giving from the positive wellsprings of who we are. We move on, accepting the lack of guaranteed, constructive outcomes.

Fully Invested One,
I, too, am meant to be as present,
as kind, and as concerned as you are.
And I, too, cannot cling to certainty
or persist in an indulgent desire to know
if I have made a difference for others.

Today: I act positively on behalf of someone and
forego the need for gratification.

Wednesday

Bringing a Sword

> Do not think that I have come to bring peace to
> the earth; I have not come to bring peace, but
> a sword.
>
> —Matthew 10:34

What is Jesus suggesting? Surely not anything literal. Yet his statement bears tough implications: anyone who takes his guidance seriously will undoubtedly have a price to pay, one that may slice through cultural and societal norms, even separate one from Church law. Jesus welcomed persons on the margins of life, seeming to prefer them to a more acceptable and genteel community. In our day this would indicate being with and accepting people who are on the low rung of admiration. This could include "the poor"—people who have not been able to clear a way out of debt or who regularly rely on governmental assistance—or persons who've been incarcerated, or those who enter a country's borders seeking asylum. Relationships have been sliced apart when a family or church member admits to being a part of the LGBTQ community. No wonder Jesus used the symbol of a sword. Reaching out to marginalized persons can cut a deep divide between ourselves and those we love.

Personally, I much prefer peace to division, keeping my mouth shut to speaking up. When I do indicate support on the behalf of disdained people, or when I encourage privileged persons like myself to have compassion, I'm uncomfortable knowing someone may be picking up "the sword" against me because of my words. But discomfort and fear ought not stop me from following the course of Jesus.

Disrupter of Complacency,
when I am hiding behind quavering fears
and lack the firm courage to do what is right,
drag my reluctance out of the murky shadows;
walk tall with me as I go beyond my comfort zone
and hold my hand so I do not falter on the way.

Today: I evaluate my attitude and speech regarding marginalized persons.

Thursday

THE EFFECTIVENESS OF ONE PERSON

> And again [Jesus] said, "To what should I compare the kingdom of God? It is like yeast that a woman took and mixed in with three measures of flour until all of it was leavened."
>
> —Luke 13:20–21

At eighty-two, my sister-in-law still bakes several loaves of bread every week. I marvel at how she kneads a lump of sticky dough with flour until it's smooth, then puts it in a pan to sit quietly so it can increase in size. The interaction of ingredients and yeast causes a little miracle to materialize as the dough rises. What pleasure when the delicious loaves of bread are taken out of the oven. No wonder Jesus chose the metaphor of yeast when he spoke about the kingdom of God. Whether using the image of yeast or a tiny mustard seed growing into a tree, he urged his listeners to trust in their ability to be instruments of bringing about greater love through their ordinary deeds.

The kingdom of God (the realm of love) grows by seemingly small and insignificant endeavors like tiny granules of yeast activating an astounding transformation. Just as the yeast's hidden power to raise bread dough, or a mustard seed's capability of growing into a large tree, so also our hardly noticeable loving actions of each day can motivate surprising transformation. Let us remember that we most often contribute to the realm of love not by grandiose gestures but by those tedious or unacknowledged efforts to be kind, forgiving, patient, and faithful to our commitments.

Hidden Source of Transformation,
you are the yeasty source of grace
mixing into the dough of daily life.
Thank you for being a vital catalyst
for ongoing development within myself
and those whom I encounter.

Today: I move through the day intent on the loving quality of my actions.

Friday

COME TO ME

Come to me, all you that are weary and are carrying heavy burdens, and I will give you rest.
—Matthew 11:28

What distresses you now? What feels like a heavy weight unable to be lifted from your life? Some difficulty of your own or that of another? Perhaps you are feeling fine and at peace with no worries or concerns. If so, you are one of the exceptions in this distraught world we live in. It's quite unusual for someone to be alive and avoid facing an issue that weighs heavily on the mind and heart. At one time or another, and sometimes quite often, we require the kind of rest and release that can't be taken care of through a long night's sleep. Whether heading off to a demanding job with relentless strains, in a retirement center where each day requires considerable energy to care for self, or in any situation that causes weariness of spirit, a weighty load can deter us from the joy and contentment we long to have.

However we are currently experiencing life, let us focus on the heartening invitation Jesus gave to his disciples and now extends to us: "Come to me. Come and I will teach you how to carry peace within you. Let me be a part of your life. Come to me and lean on my love. If you accept this invitation, your burdens may not go away, but they will feel lighter and more manageable. I have strength enough to see you through to better days."

Source of Easing Burdens,
I give the heavy, disquieting aspects
of my life into your promised care.
Revive my trust that the weightiness
will be reduced when I come to you
with burdens that weary my spirit.

Today: I lessen my grip on one of my burdening
concerns.

Saturday

THE LOWEST PLACE

> When you are invited, go and sit down at the
> lowest place, so that when your host comes, he
> may say to you, "Friend, move up higher."
> —Luke 14:10

Valerie Kaur, author of *See No Stranger*, entered Yale law
school with the hope of assisting impoverished citizens.
She soon discovered that "many of our classmates pur-
sued (jobs) because they were markers of success, not
because they advanced a vision of how they wanted to
serve the world. There was even a name for it—'pres-
tige-chasing.'"[1] Never-ending attractions cajole people
like this to seek the top place of recognition and admiration. Indicators of this kind of inflated ego show up when
we feel miffed for being left out of an honor, upset when
not being called by our name, or longing for praise even
if it's false flattery.

Taking the lowest place does not mean accepting injustice or meekly declining gratitude, feeling like a martyr, or rebuffing genuine affirmation. Every person requires fairness and praise, but not an excessive grasping for it. Being thought well of and attaining success need not be detrimental to spiritual growth, but when we push thoughtlessly or arrogantly to the head of the table with complete disregard for others waiting to be seated, then we have to change our focus and attitude. When we "know our place" and accept it, we remain peaceful even if we come in last. Not everyone can be first. Humility retains our belief in self-worth and helps us refuse to carry hardness of heart at the good fortune of someone else.

Source of Truth,
draw me away from an avid pursuit
to shine as one of the best or finest,
standing out prominently in the crowd.
Remind me often that what truly counts
is having a permanent place in your heart.

Today: I voice genuine praise to someone whom I appreciate.

SECOND WEEK OF LENT

Sunday

AS I HAVE LOVED YOU

I give you a new commandment, that you love one another. Just as I have loved you, you also should love one another. By this everyone will know that you are my disciples, if you have love for one another.

—John 13:34–35

Think about the love Jesus revealed in his relationships. He fearlessly invited inconspicuous fishermen into his heart; encouraged each person he encountered—whether a shifty tax collector or a baffled woman at a well—to be all they could be; offered forgiveness when his disciples offended or failed him; comforted the mournful and healed the ill; and trusted his dedicated followers to stand by him in his final hours of greatest vulnerability. I marvel that I have the capacity to love with this kind of generosity and compassion. So do you. Jesus would never have asked this of his disciples, or of us, unless he believed it was possible. We can trust that loving others in the way that Jesus loved is something within our reach.

Because *love one another* is a directive, this commandment might be thought of as a burdening challenge rather than the enriching opportunity it actually is. I once thought of this imperative as an iron-clad, impossible task, but now, in my later decades of life, I comprehend the benefit of truly loving one another. I have developed greater appreciation and understanding of the complexities of human nature, and I have come to see the enjoyment and satisfaction that occurs when loving as Jesus did.

Love of My Life,
I desire to keep my heart emptied
of unloving debris that slowly collects
like the splinters of caustic words
and heavy stones of unattended hurt.
Keep me drawing ever closer to you.

Today: I choose to love someone in the manner in which Jesus loved.

Monday

INHERITANCE ISSUES

Someone in the crowd said to [Jesus], "Teacher, tell my brother to divide the family heritage with me." . . . He said to them, "Take care! Be on your guard against all kinds of greed; for one's life does not consist in the abundance of possessions."

—Luke 12:13, 15

It's not surprising that someone brought this issue to Jesus and wanted him to solve it. In just one breath of mine I connected with the person insisting Jesus make his brother share his inheritance. How often money disrupts and destroys relationships, especially among family members. Relatives of mine used to be closely knit siblings until they bickered over who got what in their parents' will. Sadly, some have not spoken to one another for years. But possessiveness can pull at our hearts in situations even beyond questions of inheritance. I feel it when

I am drawn to anything material that I insist is "mine" and deserve to have. The question revolves around *why*: Why do I believe I have the right and feel a desperate need to acquire something another person has?

All sorts of things capture our minds and hearts, beyond the material, so much so that we get lost in wanting them and become disconnected from others. We can be obsessed about information someone possesses or caught in a gluttonous desire for relationships that others enjoy. We can even be overly zealous for another person's spiritual growth, wanting to gobble up any resource that suggests we could attain something comparable. A gauge for unhealthy ownership can be had by asking, "What devours my attention?" and noticing the effect this consuming desire has on oneself and others.[1]

Source of Abundance,
I will clear the path of my cravings
so that whatever I especially long for
is worthy of my enduring love for you.
Let me not stumble over trifling things
that clog the good I am able to do.

Today: I sort out in my life what causes me to
stumble on the spiritual path.

Tuesday

DO YOU WANT TO BE MADE WELL?

> When Jesus saw him lying there and knew that
> he had been there a long time, he said to him,
> "Do you want to be made well?"
>
> —John 5:6

The man had been ill for thirty-eight years when Jesus saw him and presented the above question, one that on the surface appears irrelevant. Who would not want to be cured of a serious ailment after so many years, to be free from pain and immobility? Who would not be eager to enjoy the good health others take for granted? But the question is not superfluous. Like this man, some of us have ongoing physical infirmities we desperately want to move beyond, or interior hurts that have persistently clung to us since childhood and never completely healed, even with our continued effort to treat them.

Jesus clearly knew how it is possible for someone to hang on to a long-term affliction. Sometimes old hurts and past emotional wounds tag along with us for so long that we unconsciously allow them to take up permanent residence. Nursing an old grudge, enjoying the thought of revenge, sinking into a "poor me" role, or basking in the attention of a badly bruised ego unwittingly prevent a positive response to the question, "Do you want to be made well?" A woman once told me how glad she was for her cancer diagnosis because it gave her an opportunity to finally remove herself from a caustic work situation. I often wonder if she would have said yes to the question Jesus posed.

Intentional Healer,
I come to you with what ails me—
the hurts I've sought to mend.
I place this condition in your restorative hands,
trusting you will guide me to discern
how these wounds may be healed.

Today: I reflect on my hurts and my answer to the question, "Do you want to be made well?"

Wednesday

LAMP OF THE HEART

Your eye is the lamp of your body. If your eye
is healthy, your whole body is full of light; but
if it is not healthy, your body is full of darkness.

—Luke 11:34

Of the metaphors Jesus used to describe a virtuous life,
the eye as a lamp of the body (the heart) particularly
reflects how I want to approach "seeing." The way I view
what happens in life, how I observe self and others, can
serve as a source of either understanding and connection,
or misunderstanding and disconnection. When my
seeing becomes flawed, it mars my inner vision. Then I
misapprehend or underestimate a person or situation. I
become absorbed in thoughts and feelings that block an
outlook of love. If I look through the lens of resentments
or stubborn demands to fulfill my wishes, the inner
landscape becomes distorted. Just as a cataract on the
eye's physical lens causes blurring and an inability to

detect vivid colors, my inner vision then lacks the light and lucidity it requires for true comprehension.

Jesus looked transparently at the people he met. The lamp of his heart beheld their deep-rooted virtues. His inner sight also recognized hypocrisy and a lack of compassion when these were present. He did not ignore or dismiss identifying these inadequacies. It remains a daily challenge to see with the kind of vision Jesus had. I long to have the lamp in my heart emanate a steady, clear light. Staying close to the guiding principles of gospel teachings ensures that this can happen.

Visionary of My Heart,
enlarge my capacity to see clearly
with the transparent light of your love.
When the way I look at life and others
causes the lamp within my heart to dim,
I'll make every effort to brighten that light.

Today: I am aware of the lamp in my heart and the amount of light it emanates.

Thursday

LEAVE EVERYTHING?

Peter began to say to him, "Look, we have left everything and followed you." Jesus said, "Truly I tell you, there is no one who has left house or brothers or sisters or mother or father or children or fields, for my sake and for the sake of the good news, who will not receive a hundredfold."

—Mark 10:28–30a

The words "began to say" catch my attention here. What else did disgruntled Peter plan to express? Evidently, he was turning sour about what dedication to the Way was costing him, the hard work it entailed. Although Peter was prone to exaggeration, in this case he must have been on target because Jesus quickly catches the gist of his gripe. He doesn't give Peter a chance to add to anything more. He points out that Peter can't expect to receive his reward now. He has to detach from expectations and give himself to the task at hand.

Carolyn Woo, past president of Catholic Relief Services, understands this: "We too have our attachments and desires as we take timid steps toward God. We want to embrace God's way: one of unconditional love for us, unlimited second chances for the asking, and compassion for each other. Yet why can't we have both this peaceable kingdom and the things that make us feel safe, secure and important?"[1] Yes, why can't I have it all—now? But that is like planting carrot seeds one day and expecting to harvest vegetables the next, without the daily labor of watering and weeding.

Storehouse of Promises,
now is the time for me to fully accept
that my efforts and pains are worth it.
The choices, decisions, and actions I take
will make a difference for myself and others,
eventually leading to a sense of satisfaction.

Today: I investigate my expectations about the rewards of spiritual growth.

Friday

NO HESITATION

> When he entered Capernaum, a centurion came to him, appealing to him and saying, "Lord, my servant is lying at home paralyzed, in terrible distress." And [Jesus] said to him, "I will come and cure him."
>
> —Matthew 8:5–7

Jesus did not hesitate to respond positively. He heard the urgency and concern in the centurion's voice and was ready to go and assist. I think of the centurion in this story as someone who shows up and asks me to leave what I hope to accomplish on my own timetable. The readiness of Jesus implies that I am not to waver in being available to serve.

It is not uncommon for me to silently balk when I am interrupted by a spoken or unspoken request from someone, especially when I know it may well involve considerable time and emotional drain. Invariably, the centurions in my life show up when I'm feeling the most stressed about what demands to be done. Then I find myself trying to slip out of helping. The more quickly I notice this inner rebellion, the sooner I am able to dig myself out of self-orientation and accept what the situation might necessitate. I gradually turn to prayer and ask for generosity of spirit to attend to what is requested. Once I get my silent grumbling over with and choose to do what I can, I discover I'm glad to have done the right thing. I learn anew the pleasure of being able to support or ease the concerns of another person.

Compassionate Responder,
may my spirit be imbued with your readiness.
I want to be prepared and willing
to go when I am called to support others.
I will be attentive to inner resistance
when the request comes to go beyond self.

Today: I say yes to someone's spoken or unspoken need for assistance.

Saturday

Sowing Seeds in Good Soil

> Other seed fell into good soil and brought forth
> grain, growing up and increasing and yielding
> thirty and sixty and a hundredfold.
>
> —Mark 4:8

When I was in the Australian outback, a rancher asked me about my home of origin. I mentioned northwest Iowa, and he described having been there, marveling at its rich, black soil. Growing up on our farm, I had not given much thought to the kind of fields that produced lush, green rows of corn and golden stands of oats. After seeing the outback, I now understand and appreciate what we had. Soil that consists of packed clay makes it difficult for moisture and warmth to reach a seed. Rocky land keeps seeds from easily being planted and cultivated. The loose, enriching particles of moist dirt in my family's fields welcomed the seeds and encouraged their growth. No wonder Jesus spoke of finding good soil in which to plant the seeds of our valuable, faith-filled qualities so they thrive and increase.

Like the pockets of air in permeable, breathable earth, the seeds of our latent virtues require porous minds and hearts so divine grace can filter in like a soft spring rain. Good soil also consists of valuable nutrients that encourage the seeds' growth. Thus the soil of our spirit requires such enrichment as inspiring resources, daily prayer, quiet reflection, and the strengthening kinship of communal gatherings. When we review what kind of soil currently resides in the field of our hearts, may it be the "good soil" that Jesus described and affirmed.

Sower of Faith,
may the waiting soil of my Lenten heart
be open and porous to receive your love.
Each day provides endless opportunities
to grow and strengthen seeds of my virtues.
I will carefully tend to their development.

Today: I check on the quality of soil in the field of my heart.

THIRD WEEK OF LENT

Sunday

LURED AWAY

> If a shepherd has a hundred sheep, and one
> of them has gone astray, does he not leave the
> ninety-nine on the mountains and go in search
> of the one that went astray?
>
> —Matthew 18:12

While numerous incidents lead us astray, some of the most powerful ones involve negative thoughts and feelings that can swirl around: "They don't care about me." "She's just using me so she looks good." "I never do anything right." "There I go, sounding stupid again." "He didn't have to put me down like that." Upsetting, nit-picking thoughts and feelings prompt us to stray further and further away from inner harmony. These trickeries of the mind and heart ignore the Shepherd's guidance. Instead, we nurse what ails us: old resentments, a sense of unworthiness, negative illusions, and other accusatory tirades. Even when our responses to hurt are accurate and suitable, we cannot allow them to steal peace away from us by continually ruminating about them. The more we indulge in these unconstructive reactions and wander around in negativity that saps our energy and sense of self-worth, the less we sense being embraced by the Shepherd's care and unconditional love waiting to draw us nearer to his heart.

My experience of being found and returning to the flock of peace occurs when I focus more on what is good in my life and less on what upsets me. When I release what plagues my thoughts and emotions and turn toward Love guiding me, I find my way home to peace once again.

Guardian of My Soul,
when negative thoughts and feelings
allure me away from inner harmony,
you wait to lead me home to peace,
back to where your love is stronger
than anything trying to lead me astray.

Today: I am mindful of where my thoughts and
feelings lure me.

GRATITUDE AT A DEEPER LEVEL

And as they went, they were made clean. Then one of them, when he saw that he was healed, turned back, praising God with a loud voice. He prostrated himself at Jesus' feet and thanked him. . . . Then [Jesus] said to him, "Get up and go on your way; your faith has made you well."

—Luke 17:14–16, 19

Jesus does not respond to the healed leper's thank-you with "You're welcome." Instead, he commends the man for his faith—an interior movement involving a relationship between the Healer and the healed. Faith drew the leper back to Jesus, initiating gratitude not only for the restoration of his wounded flesh, but a recognition of Jesus's compassionate attention. I can imagine how the reality of this relationship slid into the man's mind as he walked away and became astounded at the disappearance of his disease. Perhaps he thought, "Something much greater than a physical change happened to me. A man I never knew cared about me. He tended to my wretched life of misery for no other reason than to offer his generous kindness. I sense the holy in him. It is this presence that attracts and inclines me to return and thank him for it."

This story of the ten lepers guides my response when unexpected and valuable incidents take place. Gratitude for my benefits naturally pours forth from prayer because of what has happened. Like the grateful leper, I hope I'm equally drawn to the Spirit of Kindness whose love ushers forth the blessings I receive.

Ever-Present Healer,
when I recognize the good fortune
of something that occurs in my life,
I will turn to you as the healed leper did
and speak gratitude for your kindness,
remembering you, source of my blessings.

Today: I give thanks for the ways in which I have
grown spiritually.

Tuesday

LOVE YOUR ENEMIES

But I say to you that listen, love your enemies.
—Luke 6:27

I'm glad Jesus did not say, "*Like* your enemies." Liking someone involves feeling a positive attraction and enjoyment about them. Not everyone presents appealing qualities, and some are unsafe persons who have the ability to hurt us if we allow them into our lives. The surface qualities and destructive behaviors of certain individuals disturb my equanimity. Their actions plummet my heart into caution and fear. I cannot manage *liking* these people, nor do I have to do so. But I *can* love them because divine love insists that I not despise them nor deliberately wish them any injury. The Way requires me to believe in the core goodness at the heart of those who exist as enemies—persons or groups whose actions deliberately attempt to harm others or myself.

Clarence Jordan, scripture scholar and author of *Cotton Patch*, puts it this way: "Don't tell me Jesus didn't know about enemies that were bad and unlovable. He knew them quite well. He knew what they'd do to you. He knew they'd come out and hang you on a cross if you loved 'em. But he still says you're going to have to love them."[1] That certainly sums up the difficult obligation to love our enemies. So when I feel disturbed, angry, or fearful about those who act unjustly or with cruelty, I can turn toward the deep well of love where Jesus assures us we each find a home in the divine heart.

———————————————

Lover of All,
I hope that I am ready to expand my approach,
to cast aside the stiff armor of a fearful heart
and unlatch the iron lock on compassion.
Move me away from having to "like" others
and open up my storage box of a love like yours.

Today: I make an effort to deliberately love someone I dislike or fear.

Wednesday

BE PERFECT?

Be perfect, therefore, as your heavenly Father
is perfect.

—Matthew 5:48

Long ago I received a phone call from a stranger who
immediately yelled at me. The reason? Because I mentioned in one of my books how attracted I was to the
possibility of becoming a saint. He hissed, "Who do you
think you are?" That question shook loose anything in
me that savored being better than others. It also aided me
to rethink what I meant by "saint." I was certainly not
expressing a desire to be *perfect* or among the canonized.
That word "perfect" has led too many well-meaning people away from a healthy spirituality into a crippling view
of their self-worth or, more damagingly, into scrupulosi-
ty. "Be perfect" is an inaccurate translation; the original
phrase actually refers to "being whole or complete." To
strive to be holy, or to "be a saint," is far from acting like

a do-gooder or a goody-two-shoes, aiming to get everything right and look pious. Rather, the desire to be holy involves orienting ourselves toward the north star of the gospels, with the wisdom of Jesus to guide us. When we do this, we move in the direction of being our truest, most whole and authentic selves.

Fr. James Martin writes that "holiness is something that God does with us, or in us. . . . But we must first desire it. We must open the door to God's activity within us."[1] John of the Cross, who *is* an official saint, suggested that at death we will not be asked if we were perfect. Rather, we will be asked, "Did you love well?"

Holy One,
you do not require that I take on
every quality of your pure goodness,
but you do insist that my daily life
reflects the generosity of your love.
I desire to orient myself in that direction.

Today: I make a deliberate effort "to love well."

Thursday

STAY AWAKE

Keep awake therefore, for you do not know on
what day your Lord is coming.

—Matthew 24:42

Imagine being in a sound sleep and jolted awake by a booming clap of thunder, a piercing ambulance siren, or a phone's persistent ringing. Something comparable occurs when a tumultuous event abruptly interrupts a serene life. Daily routine and everyday relationships are no longer taken for granted. Rather than having this undesirable awakening, how much better to enter life each day with a curious, grateful spirit. Death or serious illness may arrive unexpectedly, and what sorrow to think we have missed a good portion of life's vitality because we allowed ourselves to grow drowsy with lassitude and disregard.

When Hall of Fame quarterback Terry Bradshaw was interviewed about his experience of having bladder and skin cancer, he admitted this was a big wake-up call, especially when he learned how serious the skin cancer was. Bradshaw fortunately recovered from those cancers. When asked how he was doing, he said that he didn't know if he would live a long time or if he would die tomorrow, but he was going to live his life with as much joy and aliveness as he could every day.[1] And isn't this what being awake and being prepared means—to be as fully in touch with the most vital part of our life, our relationship with the Holy One? This awareness then affects the rest of our life and allows us to enter each day with a profound appreciation for all that we've been given and to find there some happiness, some wonderment, some astoundingly simple and beautiful things to be savored with gratitude.

Awakened One,
shake loose what sleeps within my spirit
and causes me to avoid being fully alive.
When I am overly busy and too saturated
to imbibe from the wonders of daily life,
sharpen my alertness to what truly counts.

Today: I become more conscious of what needs
awakening in my life.

Friday

LOSE AND FIND LIFE

Then Jesus told his disciples, "If any want to become my followers, let them deny themselves and take up their cross and follow me. For those who want to save their life will lose it, and those who lose their life for my sake will find it."

—Matthew 16:24–25

This counsel of Jesus involves more than a recommendation. It's a requirement if one chooses to follow the Way. Whether losing self happens voluntarily or involuntarily, we are continually called to be more than we now are. There's more to learn, to love, and to live. There's also more to leave behind. The interior features that compose who we think we are hide much that is yet to be revealed. John Kirvan points this out in *God Hunger*: "Some part of us has to die if we are to live. And the part of us that must go will not be some extra that we could easily and joyfully do without. It will certainly be something that we are clinging to with all our energy because we have come to believe that it is the source of our happiness, our lives."[1]

Each of us has strongholds of identity within ourselves. We naturally resist being deprived of them. Certain features stick to us like Gorilla Glue. Yet, these very things prevent an unhampered ability to love with the fullness of our virtuous capacity. When we're resistive to inner change and growth, it's time to allow something more to be eliminated from the fortress of our presumed self.

———————————————

Strength of My Faith,
when I sense an insistent pull within me
to leave behind what needs to depart,
I will gain courage from your wise guidance.
I choose to relinquish what has to be set aside
so I can be a more authentic disciple of Love.

Today: I loosen my grip on some part of my life
that I've been holding too tightly.

Saturday

AT THE TABLE OF THE UNWANTED

But when you give a banquet, invite the poor,
the crippled, the lame, and the blind. And you
will be blessed, because they cannot repay you.
—Luke 14:13–14a

Some of those who enter the "banquet of heaven" are undoubtedly the ones I do not expect to be there. That's really not surprising. Jesus chose to welcome persons on the sidelines, the unacceptable ones whom the "more conventional" and "properly bred" think less of and tend to shun. One Lent I chose to deliberately place myself among people I either did not feel comfortable being around or whom I did not enjoy. I tried my best to go toward everyone with a welcoming spirit. I engaged in this practice at gatherings or when shopping. I also did so during prayer when I thought of certain people I gauged to be unpleasant.

When I felt like turning away from others, I remembered the banquet from this gospel and turned toward them instead, albeit sometimes reluctantly and having to give myself a whopping push in that direction. I discovered how valuable it is to sit at the table of the unwanted. I learned how smug and patronizing I can be. I was humbled by realizing I was the one unwelcome by some who sat there. I felt a common bond in knowing all of us had been wounded in some way. We were the poor, crippled, and lame. Some adverse aspect prevented each of us from being all we could be. No wonder we all sat at the same table.[1]

Gracious Host,
if I intend to sit at the table with you,
I will soon learn that it's not just us two.
There also sit the persons I prefer to avoid;
you welcome them as much as you do me.
I pray to be gladly present at your table.

Today: I welcome someone I dislike to the table
of my heart.

Fourth Week of Lent

Sunday

UNDERGOING GREAT SUFFERING

From that time on, Jesus began to show his disciples that he must go to Jerusalem and undergo great suffering at the hands of the elders and chief priests and scribes, and be killed, and on the third day be raised.

—Matthew 16:21

How did Jesus "show his disciples" the suffering that awaited him? Did he sit down and have a heart-to-heart talk? Did he, perhaps, review what he taught them in the past about the wheat seed having to fall into the ground and die before it brought forth new life? Did he speak about the pain involved? What must it have been like for those who set their hearts so completely on him to hear this news? Matthew's gospel tells us in the verse following the one above that Peter took Jesus aside "and began to rebuke him," refusing to accept this drastic reality.

Who can blame Peter? It was just too much for him to take in, as it is for us when we hear the kind of suffering ahead for us or someone we dearly love. When I am distressed, the hurt is all I can focus on. I can't get beyond the pain to emotionally embrace how I might grow spiritually and become more compassionate. This is where faith comes in. I can grow through suffering by trusting that life stretches beyond death, healing beyond hurt, peace beyond what disturbs equilibrium. Someone has been there before us and lived the truth of this reality. His name is Jesus.

Wounded One,
with what courage and determination
you made your way to the hill of Calvary.
Thank you for assuring your disciples
and all of us who suffer on our journey
that Good Friday does not have the last word.

Today: I recall ways that I have grown through what I have suffered.

Monday

DROPPING THE STONES

Let anyone among you who is without sin be
the first to throw a stone at her.

—John 8:7b

Jesus knew from his ministerial experience what it was
like to be humiliated in public. When he stood teaching
before others, he heard derisive disagreement; when he
prepared to heal the sick, he did so in spite of those who
mocked his ability to do so. Thus it is not surprising that
Jesus defended the woman accused of adultery by the
village men holding killing-stones in their hands. When
they made this woman "stand before all of them" (Jn 8:3),
her pain surely swept through the heart of Jesus. That's
when he turned toward the men's bogus superiority and
reminded them matter-of-factly that no one goes through
life with a perfect record of behavior. Every person makes
poor choices and gives in to wrongdoing.

The woman dragged to the center of condemnation could be any one of us. So could the men ready to wield a verdict. I know for certain either one could be me. Just about the time I'm sure I'd never kill someone, I find myself wishing a criminal would receive the death penalty for a heinous crime; or when I believe I'm not the greedy type, I look at my bookshelves and see how many treasures I'm unwilling to part with. The more honestly I admit to a less-than-perfect record, the more quickly I can throw down my accusations and better-than-thou attitude and respond with compassion as Jesus did.

Protector of the Disgraced,
your gaze reaches into the deepest regions
and furthest corners of the human heart,
seeing both goodness and deficiency.
Remind me often of these mutual traits
that exist in myself and in every person.

Today: I drop any accusatory stones that I may be holding.

Tuesday

IS IT WORTH PATCHING?

> He also told them a parable: "No one tears a piece from a new garment and sews it on an old garment; otherwise the new will be torn, and the piece from the new will not match the old."
>
> —Luke 5:36

Even the best-quality socks eventually become thin or develop a hole in the toes and heels. I've mended many a pair only to find a few months later how the stitching has pulled away from the remaining sock. While people today throw away clothes instead of patching them, in Jesus's time mending a garment was commonplace. He knew how this metaphor would relate to his listeners who did not have easy access to purchasing new items. They would understand his insistence on being open to fresh approaches for growing in one's faith and other personal development.

Stop patching, and take on something new—this is what we are asked to do time and again when theology, science, historical discoveries, and other disciplines present knowledge that disrupts what we've considered to be "the final answer." Uncovered truths require us to change how we live or to discard certain ideas about self, others, and God that we have acquired and considered to be absolute. It's much more comfortable to stay in the present mode even if it's not life-giving, or to adapt just a tiny bit, rather than feel ill at ease with a different approach to a belief or a mindset. Even so, Jesus insists: "If you want to grow, *stop patching*."

Guide of New Pathways,
when I feel hesitant to move beyond
fading beliefs and unmendable outlooks,
lead me past indecision and reluctance.
I hope to travel forward with confidence,
to leave behind what is no longer patchable.

Today: I search my beliefs and attitudes to see
what I might need to stop patching.

DO NOT WORRY

Therefore I tell you, do not worry about your life, what you will eat, or about your body, what you will wear. For life is more than food, and the body more than clothing. . . . And can any of you by worrying add a single hour to your span of life?

—Luke 12:22–23, 25

Do not worry? Did those listening to Jesus whisper among themselves, "What, not be anxious? Is he joking?" But, of course, Jesus was not jesting. He knew that fretting does not change a thing or lessen a troubling situation. As much as I want to trust this guidance, I still occasionally have one of those nights where I wake up plagued with questions: "What if . . . ? How can . . . ? Why did I . . . ?" After considerable tossing and turning, eventually I remember all I need to do is set aside whatever troubles me and surrender myself into the Holy One's care. Soon after this, a restful sleep returns.

While apprehensions arise that we can't change, we still have the ability to decide how to respond. We can avoid rehashing problems with no immediate solution. We can cease trying to repair what is not ours to fix and release our efforts to change outcomes that prove impossible to alter. Underneath worry is the desire to control life and have it go as we insist it should go. The next time anxieties threaten your sleep or slurp up your precious daytime energy with constant apprehension, take the advice of Jesus and cease obsessing about the inner turmoil.

Foundation of Trust,
how astutely you were able to observe
and find lessons for our human nature.
The next time worry overtakes my peace
I will remember the wisdom you taught
and relinquish what is beyond my control.

Today: I allow my worries to fly away like a bird
winging freely in the sky.

Thursday

PERFORMING GOOD WORKS

They do all their deeds to be seen by others.
—Matthew 23:5

Jesus refers to the religious teachers of his time when he speaks about people who tell others how they ought to live and what they should be doing, while they themselves do not practice their dogged exhortations. Notice the words that Jesus uses in describing this phoniness: "seen by others." Those words speak loudly about the incentive for which something is done. Performers want to be noticed, to affect the audience in a way that meets the group's expectations, along with generating personal satisfaction. For professional acting this purpose is noteworthy, but not if the person is intent on a religious practice or on doing some action of supposed benefit. I wonder if the scribes and Pharisees realized how they were just "putting on a show" for others to admire, how there existed a wide divergence between what they displayed to the public and how they actually lived their private lives. Had they become so accustomed to performing that their actions developed into an oblivious habit?

I know my ego can be a sly, sneaky character leading me astray. If I do not keep an eye on it, I can also fall into the need to be "seen by others." I am continually called back through the Spirit's guidance to look closely at the reasons for why and what I do. Sometimes the truth hurts, but it opens up the path toward spiritual integrity and clears away the contamination that mars true motivation.[1]

Source of Inspiration,
thank you for the numerous times
you have led me to reach out to others.
May my intentions be free of self-promotion
and solely for the sake of another's good,
devoid of motivations to be a performer.

Today: I am attentive to what motivates my religious practices and daily actions.

Friday

THE COSTLY PEARL

> The kingdom of heaven is like a merchant in search of fine pearls; on finding one pearl of great value, he went and sold all that he had and bought it.
>
> —Matthew 13:45

The Pearl of Divine Love attracts me—but the price of it, not so much. However, I cannot have one without the other. Since my early twenties I've been longing to have that Pearl—a dedicated relationship with the Holy One. As a young member of the Servants of Mary community, when I learned how to meditate I felt the greatest urge to set my heart on this truest of loves. I soon learned this desire is not some romantic yearning. Rather, a true-love relationship develops through choices I am required to make. I trust I have found the beloved Pearl, but I'm still "selling" what I have from my stockroom of unruly distractions. Each choice I make to set aside what keeps me from genuine love lessens that stockpile of self-oriented endeavors and strengthens my heart's focus on the Pearl.

In Mary Oliver's poem "Hum," she describes worker bees, how dedicated they are to the hive and the queen bee. They give themselves tirelessly in gathering sweetness from the "cups of flowers." This activity engages the complete focus of the bees, one that Oliver suggests is based on a love "almost too fierce to endure."[1] The worker bee in me also has to do more than buzz around in order to give myself with that much determination to unite with the Pearl.

Pearl of Great Price,
I desire to choose your enduring love
as the central aim of my heart and life.
When challenging situations require me
to move beyond self for the sake of others,
I will respond as completely as I am able.

Today: I turn my attention to the Pearl and pay
   the price of going beyond self.

Saturday

READY TO GROW?

> As they were going along the road, someone
> said to him, "I will follow you wherever you
> go." And Jesus said to him, "Foxes have holes,
> and birds of the air have nests; but the Son of
> Man has nowhere to lay his head."
>
> —Luke 9:57–58

Jesus was too young to recall the hurried journey to Egypt
his parents took when they feared for his life. He might
have remembered the arduous departure from there when
they returned and settled in Nazareth. And he most surely
carried the memory of the trip to the Temple when he was
twelve. But the last three years of his ministry when he
was constantly on the move must have been especially
significant for Jesus. He used this pilgrim experience as a
metaphor in response to the eager person ready to follow
him. By referring to the lack of a settled place for himself,
Jesus was clear that his teachings were not about nesting.

He challenged the would-be disciple about a readiness to move on from whatever held him back in order to fully participate in Jesus's transformative work.

Followers of the gospel teachings are not required to live out of a suitcase, but we will most surely be continually on the move interiorly if we intend to live those teachings with depth and authenticity. A natural urge to hold back arises when the going gets tough, when loving others feels way too demanding, when working for justice calls for further commitment, and when there's still another person to forgive. There's always more growing to do.

Mover of the Heart,
I renew my readiness to give my all
in living your teachings as best I can.
When I want to nest and stop growing,
nudge me with a boost of your love
so that I stay close to you, the Way.

Today: I listen quietly in prayer for how I am currently being led to "follow."

FIFTH WEEK OF LENT

Sunday

THE SPACE BETWEEN HURT AND FORGIVENESS

> If you remember that your brother or sister has something against you, leave your gift there before the altar and go; first be reconciled to your brother or sister, and then come and offer your gift.
>
> —Matthew 5:23–24

On more than one occasion Jesus emphasized the requirement of forgiveness. Some persons appear to forgive readily by mouthing, "I forgive you" or "Please forgive me," while secretly carrying antipathy that rubs the heart raw for years. Others let that space between leaving the gift at the altar and going to be reconciled to stretch into decades before making the effort to mend what tore the relationship apart. Personalities and life experiences affect how and when one has enough courage and humility to approach the possibility of forgiveness. While these features might be valid reasons for the wide space of alienation, they can be leaned on so heavily that valuable years of serenity are wasted.

Through several decades I resisted asking for pardon until one day I came to understand the peace that follows "Please forgive me." I learned how an immense relief accompanies the joy of knowing no more division exists between myself and the one I intentionally or unintentionally offended. When we forgive, the other person may not want to resume the relationship, but in our hearts we willingly lift the lid off of our coffined love. It is then that we are free to move on with an open heart, knowing we have passed through the challenging space between the altar and the hurt we caused.

Generous Forgiver,
if I expect my endless wrongdoings
to be swept away with your pardon,
then I choose to use my graced fortitude
to enter into that uncomfortable space
of asking to be forgiven for the hurt I cause.

Today: I take another step toward asking to be
forgiven and forgiving.

Monday

AN ABILITY TO ENDURE SUFFERING

By your endurance you will gain your souls.
—Luke 21:19

Following a warning to his disciples about their being arrested and persecuted in the future, Jesus guides them toward this impending suffering by assuring them they have the resilience required to "gain their souls." An alternate translation of this guidance reads: "By your perseverance you will secure your lives."[1] In other words, what the disciples endure in their suffering does not have to destroy their inner life of faith. Through what they have to bear, they can develop more wholly the virtuous essence dwelling in their being. They will learn that they have the firmest faithfulness, the sturdiest ability to go beyond self for the sake of another, and the hardiest resilience to follow the Way even when it seems this possibility is absurd.

None of us desires suffering of any kind, yet we cannot escape it in one form or another. Some sufferings are so intense that they overpower our ability to do anything but cry out for relief. With other travails we manage to remember and act out of a trust that we are much stronger than we think we are. I've observed this in people whose remarkable perseverance sustained them against tremendous odds when they felt unable to survive their hurts. This capacity to lean on the Crucified One, who believed in his disciples' resilience to withstand suffering, gives us the courage to do likewise. With this hope, we move step by step through unwanted distress until we recover our inner peace.

Resilient One,
you encouraged your disciples to persevere
regarding the future they would be facing.
Please lead me to this hope when I am hurting.
Assure me that I have the gift of inner resilience
when adversities threaten to overpower me.

Today: I entrust what distresses me into the care
of the Resilient One.

Tuesday

MERCY NOT SACRIFICE

And as he sat at dinner in the house, many tax collectors and sinners came and were sitting with him and his disciples. When the Pharisees saw this, they said to his disciples, "Why does your teacher eat with tax collectors and sinners?" . . . [Jesus] said, " . . . Go and learn what this means, 'I desire mercy, not sacrifice.'"

—Matthew 9:10–13

It is surely easier to resist eating a favorite food than it is to openly and kindly approach a person whose way of life differs considerably from mine. In the past I would not have been comfortable engaging in a conversation with a pony-tailed, leather-garbed, heavily bearded motorcyclist. That is, until I learned that these people whom I had moved outside the picture of benevolence were the very ones who contributed funds to the bereaved and stopped to assist stranded motorists while all the "good people" drove by.

I've noticed how almost every time I mention "immigrants" and support them in my publications, someone writes to assail me with comments like, "If you love them so much, why don't you go back with them to their own country?" This castigation seems quite similar to the one the Pharisees raised. However, I'm not wagging a finger at anyone but myself. I can still feel ill at ease with certain groups. But when I catch myself with this discomfort, I move toward mercy sooner. If I am to honestly follow the Way, I will be with people different than myself with as much openness of heart as Jesus had.

Heart of Mercy,
teach me about the growing I've yet to do
when it comes to being with the people
who do not match my notion of "good."
I pray that your gift of mercy reaches me
when I, too, am in need of this kindness.

Today: I pause to clear my heart of any castigations residing there.

Wednesday

Built on Rock

Everyone who hears these words of mine and acts on them will be like a wise man who built his house on rock. The rain fell, the floods came, and the winds blew and beat on that house, but it did not fall, because it had been founded on rock.

—Matthew 7:24–25

When I was ten years old, I watched workmen fill the basement walls of our new house with concrete. I marveled how it hardened into a solid foundation upon which our family home was then built. At the same time, the strong underpinnings of my faith were being laid through our family's religious beliefs and my education at a rural Catholic school. Since then I've had endless reasons to be grateful for this bedrock upon which my spirituality has not only survived but grown. That foundation sustained me when situations such as death swept away loved ones, when my religious faith threatened to crumble with the disillusionment of an imperfect Church, and when people I believed in proved to be weak. But my faith did not disintegrate. Its foundation held strength enough to remain standing.

What about you? Where did your foundation of faith begin? Where has it led you? How has it supported you? Has your faith ever developed some unsteady cracks during stormy weather? I'm confident you've learned, as I have, that if we make an effort to maintain our relationship with the Holy One, the walls of a sturdy faith can withstand the heavy winds threatening our spiritual demise.

Sustainer of Faith,
when the foundation of my inner home
begins to wobble and become unstable,
assure me that I have enough strength
to endure what happens to come my way.
Once again, I place my utmost trust in you.

Today: I review my foundation of faith and give thanks for how it supports me.

GO AND DO LIKEWISE

"And who is my neighbor?"

—Luke 10:29b

Jesus answers this question by telling the story of someone stripped, robbed, and left "half dead." Two persons pass by and look the other way. Then a Samaritan, an outsider, kindheartedly assists the wounded individual. Jesus concludes, "Which of these three, do you think, was a neighbor to the man who fell into the hands of the robbers?" The questioner replies, "The one who showed him mercy." To which Jesus responds, "Go and do likewise" (Lk 10:36–37).

Maureen H. O'Connell stresses "doing likewise" when she encourages us to reinterpret the road to Jericho in our current context of globalization: "Samaritanism in an age of globalization demands that we recognize the connection between our ability to travel comfortably, if not prosperously, on our way and others' inabilities to even climb out of roadside ditches. It requires that we see our connection between our privilege and the under-development of others and our inability to perceive injustices and others' perpetual experiences of them."[1]

Those challenging lines lead me to ponder: Who are the wounded ones in my life? Whom do I dismiss, step around, and avoid if at all possible? Which wounded persons remind me too much of my own hurts, the invisible ones that chafe the heart and weary the mind? When have I stopped by the hurt of others and bound up their wounds by my listening presence, or by deliberate attentiveness to their physical needs?

Neighbor to One and All,
awaken my heart to live in a kindly way.
Take me to persons who are wounded
so they may benefit by my caring presence.
Stir within my vigilant self a daily desire
to care for others on the roadside of life.

Today: I will "go and do likewise" by responding
compassionately to someone hurting.

Friday

TEND TO YOUR OWN BUSINESS

> Peter turned and saw the disciple whom Jesus
> loved following them. . . . When Peter saw him,
> he said to Jesus, "Lord, what about him?" Jesus
> said to him, "If it is my will that he remain until
> I come, what is that to you? Follow me!"
> —John 21:20, 21–22

Jesus could just as well have responded to Peter's question by saying, "Tend to your own business." Was it genuine concern, simple curiosity, a silent desire to control the situation, or something else that rested beneath Peter's question? We'll never know. However, his query supplies us with a good reminder to be careful about interfering with someone else's life by boldly inserting ourselves into it.

Being gossipy, prying, or spreading rumors can get us into a peck of trouble and even go so far as to ruin a fine relationship. Rather than having to know all the details about another person's illness, future plans, or any other personal matter, it behooves us to ask ourselves why we have a need to glean that information. Most often, it's best to entrust other people into God's providence instead of wedging our way into their private lives. St. Katherine Drexel got it right when she wrote, "It is a lesson we all need—to let alone the things that do not concern us. [God] has other ways for others to follow him; all do not go by the same path. It is for each of us to learn the path by which [God] requires us to follow."[1]

Guardian of My Soul,
when too much curiosity absorbs my mind
and my thirst for details grows too strong,
direct me toward what truly matters in life.
Let me heed the wise advice given to Peter:
"I'll take care of things. Just follow me."

Today: I am careful to respect other people's personal boundaries.

Saturday

Many Ways of Following

"Teacher, we saw someone casting out demons in your name, and we tried to stop him, because he was not following us." But Jesus said, "Do not stop him; for no one who does a deed of power in my name will be able soon afterward to speak evil of me. Whoever is not against us is for us."

—Mark 9:38–40

When a regular participant at our monthly poetry gathering casually referred to herself as an atheist, I was absolutely astounded. Her values resonated with Christianity. For the five years of our acquaintance, I pictured her as an outstanding, active member of a local church. Knowing of her compassion for impoverished people and her dedication to lessening society's injustice led me to this conviction. I thought, "Much of what she obviously believes and practices parallels the guidance Jesus gives to those of us who follow the Way."

I have often experienced this type of spiritual kinship. It encourages me to improve my Christian faith when I'm with persons of other religious traditions or those who have no formal religious beliefs. I look for threads of commonality in our approach to morality and in our concerns for alleviating global suffering. Although we might differ considerably in regard to tenets of faith that influence us, I gain confidence in knowing we are on the journey together. When I am tempted to think my way of spirituality is better than theirs, I remember what Jesus said to his disciples: "Whoever is not against us is for us."

Open-Minded Teacher,
when I pull back my acceptance of people
who differ in how they impart your guidance,
nudge me to sort through my adversarial view.
Widen the narrow lanes of my false insistence
when I believe my approach is the only valid one.

Today: I unite my heart with everyone who
desires good for our world.

Sixth Week of Lent
(Holy Week)

Sunday

ACCEPTANCE OF DEATH

He took the twelve aside again and began to tell them what was going to happen to him, saying, "See, we are going up to Jerusalem, and the Son of Man will be handed over to the chief priests and scribes, and they will condemn him to death."

—Mark 10:32–33

A longtime, cherished friend was diagnosed with brain cancer and given six months to live. When we spoke about this sudden and harsh verdict, Betty spoke candidly, "I've cried a lot, but I've lived a good life of eighty-two years. My faith is strong. I'm not afraid to die." Her faith found its roots in that of Jesus, who also went bravely toward his death. The gospel authors comment at least nine times about Jesus trying to let his disciples know that he would not live much longer. The disciples either recoiled at his attempt, denied it, or dismissed it as a possibility. What are we to make of their responses to Jesus's effort to prepare them for the future demise awaiting him?

The death of their strong, beloved mentor was too difficult for the disciples to imagine. This is not surprising. The truth about one's own or another's death can be difficult to comprehend and accept. Jesus went reluctantly yet willingly toward his impending death, accepting vulnerability and mortality. Betty's faith enabled her to do something similar. Unlike Jesus, she had a beloved family and longtime friends to be there with her—more than the three faithful ones standing nearby his Cross.

Companion of the Dying,
your courageous and honest assent
to the truth of your approaching death
urges me to accept my own future ending.
Be a source of strength when death nears
so I am able to surrender peacefully to it.

Today: I pray to move beyond fears or concerns I
have about my future death.

Monday

Unless the Seed Dies

Very truly, I tell you, unless a grain of wheat
falls into the earth and dies, it remains just a
single grain; but if it dies, it bears much fruit.

—John 12:24

Can you imagine yourself as a seed under a layer of soil?
What must it be like—to be pushed into the dark; to wait
and wait for moisture to slowly unwrap the tough, protec-
tive shell, for sunlight to warm and welcome it; to sense
the energy of something growing? Our spiritual growth
is much the same. Latent virtues and qualities in us await
sprouting. For this to happen, some part of us must be
shed so an unforeseen, valuable feature can be developed
in our being.

When our spirits are buried in the depths of grief,
who would expect that we might find fresh life in our
empathy for others who've suffered loss? Or that the bit-
terness we've known from a rancid betrayal could lead to

a deeper understanding of what forgiveness truly means? Or that the anger flowing like a lava stream in us since childhood abuse could shed the shell of brutal pain and rise through the dark soil of years, helping us discover how wondrously healing love can be? If we are to grow into the fullness of our personhood, we will find ourselves in the unknown dark from time to time. Faith gives us patient confidence. Hope assures us that a green shoot will rise. Love bids us to have trust that we are not alone in this process.

Companion in the Dark,
when I am like a seed in the soil
wondering if I will ever see green,
wait with me there in the silence;
grant that I may find the courage
to not give up believing in my growth.

Today: I picture some aspect of my spirituality as a seed waiting in the soil.

Tuesday

THY WILL BE DONE

"If you are willing, remove this cup from me;
yet, not my will but yours be done."

—Luke 22:42

When Jesus entered the garden of Gethsemane, he knew
death was approaching. Once again, he "walked his talk"
and entered into what was his to endure. I wonder if the
words Jesus had asked his disciples to pray pressed upon
him then. (Matthew's gospel has him saying, "Your will
be done, on earth as it is in heaven" [6:10].) That prayer
was soon to be mirrored in his fearful, blood-sweating
agony when he would plead to have the cup of suffering
taken away.

The experience of Jesus guides us when we enter into
our desolating and unwanted life events. If only we could
remember and embrace his exemplar moment when our
Gethsemane-type suffering arrives with occurrences like
the unexpected death of someone dear; a sharp ending of

a valued relationship; a painful, extended illness; a natural or financial disaster. The first response that hurriedly leaps out of us may be to question why, to blame God for what is happening, or, as Jesus did, to beg that the suffering be taken away. If suffering cannot be ended, then his yielding response becomes our prayer of acceptance: "I don't want this. But if it cannot be changed, then I am willing to accept how the future will proceed. I trust you with my life." This surrender does not lessen the intensity of the struggle, but it generates courage and faith to go forward by leaning on the Holy One's strength.

Suffering Servant of Abba,
if what I desperately long to get rid of
stubbornly refuses to budge or depart,
take me to that painful place of yours
where you knelt in agony at Gethsemane.
Wrap your strengthening love around me.

Today: I bring what I find difficult to accept and
place it in the Holy One's care.

Wednesday

ABIDE IN ME

Abide in me as I abide in you.

—John 15:4a

What a significant difference a two-letter word can make: Abide *in* me, instead of *with* me. "With" indicates being alongside someone or something—a certain separateness, whereas "in" designates unity, an intimacy or together-ness. Some biblical translations use the words "remain in me," implying having already been tucked into the divine heart. In either case, Jesus is encouraging an inner solidarity between himself and his disciples. He does so at a time when he is preparing to depart physically from them. An unshakeable love comes through his final message, a longing for those he holds dear to know and accept an assurance of his permanent affection for them.

As followers of the Way, these words reach into our lives and invite us also to abide as fully as possible in union with the divine heart. This reassuring message never grows stale. Instead, the Spirit of Jesus repeats it continually to us: *Remember you are in my heart. Stay present there no matter what happens externally. Absorb as much of my abiding presence as you can, so much so that your life becomes overflowing with my love. I will be your strength when you feel frail or unworthy. I will rejoice with you when happiness radiates within you. If you feel lost, you are never lost to me. Trust that I am in you and you are in me. There is no separation in our dedicated love for one another. Go with confidence in this permanent unity.*

Abiding Presence,
what consolation and encouragement
I receive when I consider how fully
you and I are merged in our mutual love.
I will lean on the veracity of this oneness
and allow your affection to influence my life.

Today: I place my hand over my heart, uniting
with the Holy One abiding in me.

Holy Thursday

MORE THAN A GESTURE OF SERVICE

> Having loved his own who were in the world, he loved them to the end. . . . [Jesus] got up from the table, took off his outer robe, and tied a towel around himself. . . . [He] began to wash the disciples' feet and to wipe them with the towel.
>
> —John 13:1b, 4–5

When Jesus realizes the end of his earthly life is near, he chooses an ordinary action that becomes extraordinary. This washing of feet expresses much more than a humble gesture of service. It portrays an action of immense love, assuring his disciples that a permanent, spiritual kinship exists between them and himself. He has loved them through their endless questions, misunderstandings, doubts, hesitancies, mistakes, squabbles, and foibles and never given up on them. Not once. Now Jesus bends low, takes each foot that walked many miles with him through villages, countryside, and city, and washes away the odorous grime. With this cleansing of their feet, Jesus confirms his love and his promise that he will not abandon them. Instead, he will be forever present with them through his Spirit of Love.

All of us serve in one capacity or another, oftentimes in unpretentious postures—preparing a meal, mowing a lawn, tending children's needs, serving as church greeters and ushers. All of this can be done with the same kindhearted care and dedicated love as shown in the washing of the disciples' feet. Perhaps today is the time to dust off our motivations and cleanse any lack of love we have when we extend service to others.

Beloved Foot-Washer,
how magnanimous was your deep love
that you chose to move subserviently
at the feet of each one of your disciples.
I long for my service to be that devoted,
to be shared with such profound humility.

Today: I do even the smallest act of service with
intentional love.

Good Friday

THE DARKNESS OF GOOD FRIDAY

> When it was noon, darkness came over the whole land until three in the afternoon. At three o'clock Jesus cried out in a loud voice, "Eloi, Eloi, lema sabachthani?" which means, "My God, my God, why have you forsaken me?" . . . Then Jesus gave a loud cry and breathed his last.
>
> —Mark 15:33–34, 37

When Holy Week arrives, I usually dread the Good Friday liturgy with its starkness—the somber reading of the passion and death of Jesus, a focus on the Cross, and the lack of a complete Eucharistic service. A hollow silence accompanies this austere ritual as the congregation departs. In spite of my reluctance to experience the melancholic mood, Vincent Pizzuto's astute statement in

Contemplating Christ motivates me to attend this liturgical commemoration: "We cannot live the light of Easter while flinching from the darkness of Good Friday."[1]

If I were left with only the historical memory of Jesus's death, I would miss the meaning of that darkness. I would do little more than feel sorry for his demise. The depth of Jesus's desolation restores my willingness to accept that loss and suffering may also result for me if I try to live as lovingly as he did. Christianity is about more than fuzzy, warm feelings and improved prosperity. Challenges accompany following the Way, consequences from efforts to love as generously as he did. If I am to "live the light of Easter," then I also accept living "the darkness of Good Friday," however this may manifest due to my choice to follow the Way.

Desolate Guide of My Life,
what depth of darkness enveloped you
as you cried out in pain and felt abandoned.
I ask myself today if I can be that dedicated,
to give that totally of my capacity to love,
so much so that I might be swept into darkness.

Today: I review the opportunities that have
urged me to love generously.

Holy Saturday

YOU ARE THE LIGHT

You are the light of the world. A city built on a hill cannot be hid. No one after lighting a lamp puts it under the bushel basket, but on the lampstand, and it gives light to all in the house. In the same way, let your light shine before others, so that they may see your good works and give glory to your Father in heaven.
—Matthew 5:14–16

In their grim sadness, how could followers of the Way believe they carried the light Jesus urged them to share? Grief broke apart their world, left them discouraged and heartbroken, with sparse energy to lift off "the bushel basket." We know from gospel memories that days and weeks passed before their enthusiasm revived. The love that burned in the disciples' hearts rebounded with vigor only when the Spirit of Love arrived, rekindling their hearts and bolstering their faith. Only then could they

110

trust that, yes, they *were* "the light of the world." Yes, they *could* go forth, not in spite of the tremendous loss of their Teacher, but because of it.

Now they understood about the dying seed and the new life that would follow. Now they truly believed they were meant to be carriers of Jesus's message. They trusted they had the ability to do it. Their Guide did not abandon them. Instead, he was there as the Risen Seed, ever-present in an invisible and vibrant relationship. This Light would warm their faith-filled devotion to the Way and illuminate their path.

Light of the World,
thank you for being the lamplighter
of love dwelling within my heart.
Together we can make a difference.
I draw on your graced radiance
and look forward to shining brightly.

Today: I prepare for Easter with my Light-filled
spirit ready to follow the Way.

HEAD FOR HOME

The man who had been possessed by demons begged [Jesus] that he might be with him. But Jesus refused, and said to him, "Go home to your friends, and tell them how much the Lord has done for you." . . . And [the man] went away and began to proclaim in the Decapolis how much Jesus had done for him.

—Mark 5:18–20

Have you ever been on a retreat where peace flowed abundantly into your stressed spirit, or went on a vacation where beauty astounded your weary eyes at every turn? When we experience a flood of relief, a much-needed inner restoration, or a renewed sense of grace directing us, we naturally want to cling to it, to grab hold and stay where we are for as long as possible. That is how the man possessed by demons felt when he begged Jesus to let him stay and journey with him. Mary of Magdala probably had a similar longing when she finally recognized the gardener as her beloved Teacher. Here, too, Jesus insists that Mary not cling to him but go back and tell others whom she has encountered (see Jn 20:11–17).

We have completed the six weeks of Lent. Easter has arrived. We are now to move on, to take the experience of meeting our wise and trusted Guide and go forth to share our graced renewal. It is time for us to "go home" into the families, communities, and work spaces where our restoration can breathe and affect how we intend to go about our lives.

Ever-present Guide,
I give thanks for how your persistent Spirit
walked with me through the Lenten weeks.
Now I gladly take the next step forward
to incorporate into life's hills and valleys
the valuable guidelines you've restored in me.

Today: I make a list of guiding principles I plan
to integrate as I "head home."

A Prayer for Guidance

She will guide me wisely in my actions.
—Wisdom 9:11b

Trusted Guide,
you are my Mentor and Inspiration,
my Home of good choices and decisions.
You help me search with confidence
as I find my way to inner peace.
Please gather your wisdom around me.
Guide me carefully as I make choices
about how to use my energy positively.
Place your discerning touch on my mind
so that I will think clearly.
Place your loving influence on my heart
so I will be more fully attentive

to what is really of value.

Teach me how to hear your voice,

to be aware of what is in my mind and heart,

to attend to your wisdom in those around me,

to acknowledge my intuitions and ponder my
  dreams,

to listen to the earth and all of life,

for in each piece of existence you are guiding me.

Guide of my life,

thank you for all you have given to me.

Reveal my spiritual path

and direct me as I join with you, the Way.

Lead me to inner peace and oneness with you.

Weekly Questions for Reflection

FOR PERSONAL REFLECTION AND GROUP FAITH-SHARING

Begin by choosing one of the prayers from the week. Pray it aloud. Follow this with a few minutes of quiet time to attune your mind and heart to what you experienced the past week when praying with *Jesus, Guide of My Life*. Then, proceed with the following and any other questions or insights you deem suitable to the faith-sharing conversation or your personal reflection.

As you look back over the past week, reflect:

1. Which of this week's reflections most inspired and encouraged you? Did any of the descriptions of Jesus's guidance surprise you or lead you to a new awareness?

2. Which day was most difficult for you to pray? What made it challenging?

3. Which day did you especially resonate with and appreciate?

4. Of the various forms of guidance presented this week, which are you most drawn to strengthen and put into practice? Which is toughest for you to activate?

5. If you were to choose an image, a symbol, or a song to describe praying with the week's topics, what would you choose, and why?

6. In the past, how have you experienced the teachings from this week? What effect has this made in the way you now live?

7. How would you describe your Lenten journey thus far?

8. Anything else about the reflections that you would add?

Close each time of reflection by praying another one of the prayers from the week.

For your final time of reflection on your Lenten journey, conclude by responding to this question: "How would you summarize your experience of praying with *Jesus, Guide of My Life*?"

NOTES

INTRODUCTION

1. Marcus J. Borg and John Dominic Crossan, *The Last Week* (New York: HarperCollins, 2006), 24–25.

2. Marilyn McEntyre, "Where the Eye Alights," *Give Us This Day*, July 2022, 157.

3. Vincent Pizzuto, *Contemplating Christ* (Collegeville, MN: Liturgical Press, 2018), 161.

4. St. Richard of Chichester's Prayer, https://www.lords-prayer-words.com/famous_prayers/day_by_day_lyrics_prayer_st_richard.html.

FRIDAY AFTER ASH WEDNESDAY

1. Br. Guy Consolmagno, "What We're Obliged to Do," *Give Us This Day*, November 2022, 92.

SATURDAY, FIRST WEEK OF LENT

1. Valerie Kaur, *See No Stranger* (New York: Random House, 2020), 175.

MONDAY, SECOND WEEK OF LENT

1. Joyce Rupp, "Guard Against All Greed," adapted from her reflection in *Living Faith*, July 31, 2022.

THURSDAY, SECOND WEEK OF LENT

1. Carolyn Woo, "All In," *Give Us This Day*, March 2022, 22.

TUESDAY, THIRD WEEK OF LENT

1. Clarence Jordan, "The Way God Responds," *Give Us This Day,* February 2022, 211.

WEDNESDAY, THIRD WEEK OF LENT

1. Fr. James Martin, "Learning to Pray," *Give Us This Day,* November 2022, 7.

Thursday, Third Week of Lent

1. Terry Bradshaw's experience of cancer reported in the *Daily Mail*, https://www.dailymail.co.uk/sport/sportsnews/article-11273089/Terry-Bradshaw-reveals-battled-bladder-skin-cancer-past-year.html.

Friday, Third Week of Lent

1. John Kirvan, *God Hunger* (Notre Dame: Sorin Books, 1999), 118.

Saturday, Third Week of Lent

1. Joyce Rupp, "At the Table of the Unwanted," adapted from her reflection in *Living Faith*, October 2022.

Thursday, Fourth Week of Lent

1. Joyce Rupp, "Performing to Be Seen," adapted from her reflection in *Living Faith*, August 2022.

Friday, Fourth Week of Lent

1. Mary Oliver, "Hum," *Devotions* (New York: Penguin Books, 2020), 145.

Monday, Fifth Week of Lent

1. The alternate translation is from the *New American Bible with Revised New Testament*, World Catholic Press, 1986.

Thursday, Fifth Week of Lent

1. Maureen H. O'Connell, *Compassion: Loving Our Neighbor in an Age of Globalization* (New York: Orbis Books, 2009), 1–2.

Friday, Fifth Week of Lent

1. "St. Katherine Drexel," Saint of the Day, *Give Us This Day*, March 2022, 39.

Friday, Sixth Week of Lent

1. Vincent Pizzuto, *Contemplating Christ* (Collegeville, MN: Liturgical Press), 108.

Prayer for Guidance

Adapted from Joyce Rupp, *Prayers to Sophia: Deepening Our Relationship with Holy Wisdom* (Notre Dame, IN: Sorin Books, 2010), 46–47.

JOYCE RUPP is well known for her work as a writer, retreat leader, and spiritual midwife. She serves as a consultant for the Boundless Compassion program. Rupp is the author of numerous bestselling books, including *Praying Our Goodbyes*; *Open the Door*; *Return to the Root*; *Jesus, Friend of My Soul*; and *Jesus, Companion in My Suffering*. Her award-winning books include *Boundless Compassion*, *Fly While You Still Have Wings*, and *Anchors for the Soul*. She is a member of the Servite (Servants of Mary) community.

joycerupp.com